tro	plu	re
che	fi	clo
sple	sle	cha
ky	bri	spo
bro	de	gri

ste	sha	plo
spu	twy	cle
dro	spro	tro
bre	stru	de
lu	chi	mo

fi	sle	mo
shra	dra	ri
plu	po	thry
thu	fla	re
cly	bli	po

za	stry	je
bu	e	tha
spru	sle	scra
cre	fru	gri
spro	u	o

Wilson Reading System®

Student Reader
Five

THIRD EDITION

by Barbara A. Wilson

Wilson Language Training Corporation
www.wilsonlanguage.com

Wilson Reading System® Student Reader Five

Item # SR5AB

ISBN 978-1-56778-071-0

THIRD EDITION (revised 2004)

PUBLISHED BY:

Wilson Language Training Corporation
47 Old Webster Road
Oxford, MA 01540
United States of America

(800) 899-8454

www.wilsonlanguage.com

Printed in the U.S.A.

December 2006

Step 5 Concepts

Open Syllable

5.1   Open syllable in one-syllable words, **y** as a vowel (**he**, **hi**, **shy**)

5.2   Open syllables combined with vowel-consonant-e and closed syllables in two-syllable words (**protect**, **decline**)

5.3   **y** as a vowel at the end of two-syllable words when combined with a closed syllable or another open syllable (**handy**, **pony**)

5.4   Multisyllabic words, combining three syllable types: open, closed, vowel-consonant-e (**instrument**, **amputate**)

5.5   **a** and **i** in unaccented, open syllables (**Alaska**, **indicate**)

cry	flu	ho
pro	hi	sky
ply	be	so
shy	spry	me
we	fry	by

no	sly	try
ye	go	my
fly	I	he
sty	pi	she
lo	pry	why

ne	spone	cret
plit	ste	slabe
bri	tome	gly
grome	blid	thren
bli	pute	plo

threne	blipe	cho
pru	stome	chot
quo	glip	thip
mupe	shene	chi
gam	bla	scret

1   If Ed gets a bass in this lake, then I will try to fry it.

2   My Gram went to Wisconsin with us, but she did not like to fly.

3   We expect to get this mess up by the time Mom gets home.

4   The firemen will try to put out the blaze.

5   We can make pancakes with Kendall.

6   I have no costume yet.

7   We think that Fred and his classmates have the best handshakes.

8   Did she cry at bedtime?

9   We had a splendid time at the game.

10   Let's go inspect that nest and see the bird fly.

1 I think that he is shy with Kate.

2 I wish that Tom would be less impulsive.

3 My husband is a golf pro at that club.

4 Dave had the flu; Jill spent time with him and she ended up with it.

5 Jake felt as if he would cry when he lost so much cash on his bad investment.

6 I think that the salesman was quite sly.

7 We must take steps now so that the impact will not be so bad.

8 Can you try to pry this lid off the can?

9 The thrill of the conquest made him spry.

10 If you wish to take that humdrum job, so be it.

The Sly Plan

James did not want to go to school. He was in the second grade. He did like school, but at times, he just did not wish to go. James had a sly plan. He told his mom that he had the flu.

Mom said, "My, my! Good try James, but you must go. You are an old pro with the flu trick, but I think you are well." By the time he was set for school, the bus had left. His mom had to drive him to school, then fly to get to her job on time.

behind	beside	hero
label	human	pretend
remind	rewind	select
zero	erupt	begin
protest	silent	demand

behave	yo-yo	tulip
student	spoken	skyline
unite	lilac	motel
prevent	pupil	retire
basic	rodent	locate

frozen	relax	broken
ozone	remote	robot
began	minus	siren
moment	depend	polite
request	beware	prepare

female	define	open
rotate	silo	humid
protect	minus	rerun
even	donate	myself
frequent	bonus	refund

Syllable Division: One or Two Consonants

menu	program	migrate
respect	secret	respond
reflex	declare	recline
defrost	recline	hello
predict	banjo	hotel

Syllable Division: Open or Closed

solid	open	exit
moment	robin	tulip
punish	topic	relax
result	defend	relish
polite	cabin	frozen

decode	profess	resale
relate	prolong	mucus
event	canine	divest
focus	eject	native
propel	repent	stipend

profane	Cupid	cubic
revere	crisis	feline
require	revive	profile
decal	repel	sequel
omit	lotus	bisect

bypass	basin	raven
deduct	reject	climax
item	trisect	Polish
tripod	basis	defect
elope	denote	vacate

detach	erect	erase
devote	stipend	erupt
mutate	sinus	revise
rebate	provide	python
unit	potent	proton

dilate	equate	detest
haven	dilute	stupid
zenith	yodel	edict
rebel	nylon	totem
stucco	debate	bisect

apex	elate	refine
relent	promote	revoke
depict	defect	amen
beheld	bequest	bison
befit	blatant	beget

beset	brunet	brazen
cohere	colon	crusade
cremate	crocus	cubit
debase	defile	deject
delete	delude	demise

demure	demon	derive
desire	detest	devise
elect	emit	equip
evil	evoke	fetus
haven	humane	lupine

locus	mason	obese
opal	prefab	preside
preset	presume	pagan
primate	probate	procure
profuse	propel	prudent

radon	rebuke	refuse
refute	remiss	remake
remit	resist	reset
reside	resume	retake
revise	rotund	sedan

biplane	deprive	declare
hatred	vibrate	repress
refresh	deplete	restrict
deflect	preshrunk	regret
Dacron	despite	decline

seclude	refract	hybrid
replete	restore	redress
depress	putrid	declare
deflate	deprave	detract
egress	fragrant	matrix

Final Open

ditto	bronco	stucco
solo	banjo	veto
tempo	halo	gumbo
lotto	gusto	logo
limbo	bingo	motto

Mixed Syllable Division

matron	migrant	microbe
macron	preclude	regret
regress	sacrum	vagrant
rabbi	senile	hydrate
strident	vacant	duplex

final	legal	brutal
focal	fatal	rival
vital	vocal	local
oval	total	natal
tribal	frugal	papal

Syllable Division: Open or Closed

profit	equip	rapid
valid	travel	revise
elect	toxic	sinus
comic	edit	Polish
item	detach	secure

crimope	restrimp	glestome
prestope	trymest	trumepe
clemost	floment	ploshent
streblent	ploton	frolipe
glosop	trenete	prespere

brytome	crozump	blenet
rebelt	demest	protrum
benap	triglone	tridem
flothine	grystod	stomest
delum	reflimp	glimote

1 The student could not relax until the test was complete.

2 You must protect your skin in the sun.

3 Let's relax in the basement by the fire.

4 Ms. Gannon was quite polite when she spoke.

5 We must request a refund on this dress.

6 Jim will be silent when he gets the best athlete prize.

7 Tim will deflate the raft and store it in the shed.

8 We must not disrupt the big event.

9 I will relax at the lake with Jason and David.

10 We will spend some time at that motel.

1   I admit that I like this program.

2   The lake is frozen so we can skate.

3   We cannot locate the new dentist.

4   I predict that they will elect Mr. Smith.

5   Did the students behave while I was out?

6   I hope that cat can take care of the rodents.

7   Bruno has a secret to tell Fran.

8   The class was silent when Mr. Salvo came in.

9   In a moment, I will tell you that joke.

10 We will get some tulips in April.

1   That stone home is vacant.

2   At the very last moment, Patrick sunk the basket to win the game.

3   The class will begin the spelling test.

4   This student is quite polite on the bus.

5   Robin likes that fragrant smell.

6   It is human to make a mistake.

7   We have a pupil from Hopedale in this class.

8   The Irish jig is lots of fun.

9   We must try to locate our mistakes and then fix them.

10   Eject that tape and put in this one.

1   Did Kent regret spilling his drink on the rug?

2   Jim had a wild decal on his pink van.

3   The men and women will prepare to go on strike.

4   The gold medal depended on the last program.

5   He must deduct that item from the bill.

6   We will check-in at the hotel and then go dine.

7   Tyrone prevented the dispute at the shop.

8   I wish we could escape from this humid day.

9   Bob will donate cash to the Crisis Fund.

10   Mike and Bev Fresco had a fine duplex in Boston.

1   A student in my class is in Poland on a trip.

2   We hope to prevent any problems with this contract.

3   I regret that Jeff cannot make the event.

4   Rod will have to defend his request for all that time off.

5   My dad went to the shop to demand a refund.

6   The staff can provide the help you need.

7   I cannot depend on Brad if it is a hot, humid day.

8   Bill plans to retire and devote time to the project.

9   I regret the last vote by the congress.

10   Can you donate to this program for the homeless?

1   My Spanish class elected to take the final exam.

2   I will escape to the hotel to relax.

3   This run of bad luck is depressing.

4   Did Jason deflate the raft and store it in the shed?

5   We have to repel these insects!

6   I think that this is a defect in the silk.

7   I would like to inquire about the crisis.

8   I demand that you locate the boy.

9   His hatred made him a very sad man.

10   A dog is a canine; a cat is a feline.

1   Chuck is the hero in that novel.

2   Bev will refuse the gift from Chad.

3   The mob is yelling in protest.

4   Would you like to begin the objective test?

5   Did Mr. Hopkins declare that the lake was o.k. for swimming?

6   I hope that they restore the old mill.

7   The cop must direct traffic on Brazen St.

8   We will depend on Jim to make up a motto for our club.

9   Dr. Jones will prescribe a pill for my flu.

10   The congressmen will prolong the crisis with no vote.

1   He plans to secure the vacant lot.

2   The panel will discuss vital topics for the district.

3   Ed is a migrant from Scotland.

4   Ted Mason has a strong desire to do the best job.

5   Mr. Chang is protesting the strike.

6   Jim likes to pretend that he is rich, but he is quite broke!

7   We must restrict the time that you spend under the sunlamp.

8   Sheldon did not respond to my note.

9   Why did Jane refuse to wipe the tripod?

10   You must declare the profit and file the tax form.

The Basement Mess

Mike asked his mom if he could go to the basketball game.

"That depends on your dad," she said, "He will be home at six. He told me that he had plans for you to help him in the basement."

When Mike's dad came home, Mike was quick to ask him about the game. His dad said, "Mike, the game will be lots of fun, but you made the mess in the basement. You can go to the game the moment you finish with me. I insist that you complete the task."

Mike was upset. He would miss lots of the game. He had to admit that his dad did provide some help. At last, the task was complete. Dad said that the basement was fine. Mike ran off to the game and had fun.

The Bingo Game

Kate and Mrs. Migrane went to the bingo game. The tempo of the game was quite fast. They did not relax at all! They had to focus on the call so that they did not miss a thing. The entire hall was silent. Kate just had to get a "B-nine". She did prepare to yell bingo.

As the moments went by, she could feel the climax. This was the biggest game of all. Then the call came - "B-nine." BINGO! Kate collected the five-hundred dollar prize! Not bad for a night of fun.

The Project

The boss gave Sal and Gabe a complex project. They had to devote lots of time to it. The boss had given them a profile of what they had to do. They wanted to accomplish it without lots of help. They did not relax at all.

Gabe and Sal did not stop for a moment. In five days the entire project was complete. The boss had not expected it then. He felt that the result must not be what he had wanted. Then Gabe and Sal presented the project to him. The boss was glad to see that it did fill his request. It was well done! Gabe and Sal were glad.

The Stucco Home

Jane went for a long drive. She was lost, but she did not care. She went down a small street. At the end, there was an old stucco home for sale. Jane got out to inspect it. It was such a tranquil spot! The dwelling sat at the top of a hill with stone steps up to it. She felt like this home had been made for her!

That night, Jane told her husband, Rob, about the stucco home. He felt he could predict the cost - expensive! Still, he said that he would inquire about it with her. He did like the prospect as well.

Jane made the call to the salesman. They set up a time to go see the home. Jane and Rob went but did not dare to hope. When they drove down the street, Rob felt the same as Jane: he did like the remote spot. Inside the home, Jane and Rob were in a daze. The home had been neglected, but Rob and Jane could revive it. They could expect problems from an old home like this. At last Rob did inquire about the cost. On the basis that it would require lots of work to update it, the cost was not bad. It was inexpensive for the size of the home and land.

Rob and Jane were ecstatic! Most of the time they were not impulsive, but this time, they felt that the stucco home that sat on the hill was just for them.

Jake Behaves at the Debate

The students in Mrs. Russel's debate class had to prepare for the congressmen's visit. They had to profile each congressman.

Jake had to respect the congressmen and be silent while they had their debate. Jake was not the best kid in the class, but he did behave at the event. He wanted to yell protests, but he was not rude and he did repress his comments. Despite all this, Jake did find that the class was quite good.

At the end of the debate, the kids had time to dispute the congressmen in a polite way. Jake did this well. Mrs. Russel went up to Jake and said, "You did so well! I think that you can now have a dispute and still respect the other person. You get an A for the day!"

jelly	puppy	jetty
funny	belly	buggy
lady	jolly	dizzy
plenty	happy	fifty
silly	handy	ruby

baby	penny	daddy
empty	granny	nasty
trolly	sunny	study
skinny	cozy	duty
angry	crazy	candy

pony	navy	pantry
copy	lobby	tidy
holly	ivy	taffy
puny	pansy	gravy
lazy	tiny	bunny

Tammy	Billy	Timmy
Jimmy	Wendy	Tony
Cathy	Lenny	Toby
Amy	Betsy	Sally
Molly	Sandy	Henry

holy	dandy	nifty
petty	caddy	sultry
cranny	sentry	cranky
rally	entry	daffy
petty	caddy	filly
sissy	daffy	belfry
giddy	crony	folly
canny	envy	musty
ditty	duly	shinny
shanty	eddy	zany

1   I dislike this lumpy gravy.

2   Dad will take Sandy to the ranch for a pony ride.

3   That old man is so jolly!

4   The entire cabin was so filthy that the kids had to spend the day with dust cloths and mops.

5   Betty is such a silly kid.

6   Dad demands that I empty this trash can at this moment, before I go to the game.

7   The baby got a tan on her belly.

8   Wendy was selfish with the candy, so she hid it on the top shelf.

9   Get the chestnuts in the pantry.

10   Jim must provide us with a copy of his plans.

1   Let's ride the trolly to the shopping malls.

2   The student has plenty of talent in that subject.

3   James is quite handy at the shop.

4   Jenny will smile if her daddy brings her home a puppy.

5   Tommy had plenty of cash to bring to the big event.

6   At times, that crazy kid does not behave.

7   Did Sally get dizzy from her flu shot?

8   Jimmy dislikes jelly in his donuts.

9   The baby was so tiny when she came home.

10 Sandy's ivy plant will do well in that spot.

1 Billy will caddy at that golf club.

2 Bobby and Jenny like to collect nifty things.

3 What is that nasty smell in the pantry?

4 Did Molly get the expensive ruby from Malcom?

5 The press felt it was their duty to publish all the facts in this case.

6 Mr. Jones had to depend on his staff, so he got quite angry if they did not do the job.

7 I think that Sally made a nasty comment to Jane.

8 Mr. Smith is sixty-five and still has lots of spunk so he did not wish to retire at all.

9 The moment Jane left with Stan, Jim felt his envy rise.

10 It is musty in that old cabin.

1 Mom had to prepare Molly so that she would not be cranky on their visit.

2 Jimmy will enlist in the navy and his dad hopes that he will like it.

3 Dolly made this commitment, but she is lazy and has not done it yet.

4 Jim's instinct told him not to trust the lady in his store.

5 The congressmen will debate in the lobby of the hotel.

6 I think that Mr. Kilty is happy with this effective plan.

7 That kind old man likes to cut lots of holly for his shanty.

8 James intends to close up the shop and tidy it before he goes home.

9 The boss expects this job to be complete in plenty of time.

10 The students in the lobby are quite giddy.

The Pony Ride

Betsy was five years old. She had a life-long wish to go on a pony ride. She had made this request many times. At last, her daddy came home and said, "Betsy, let's go on that pony ride."

Dad, Mom, and Betsy went for a long drive to a big ranch. Then they went to see the pony. Betsy did not run up to it. She hid behind her dad and acted shy. It took her some time to behave bravely.

At last, Betsy got on the pony. A puppy ran with the pony and Betsy had fun. On the way home, Mom said, "Let's stop to get a milk shake!"

Betsy felt it was the all-time best day of her life!

Room at the Ritz

A lady went into the lobby of the expensive Ritz Hotel. She went up to the desk and began to demand the best room in the hotel. The man behind the desk did try to be polite, but the lady did not let him respond. She became angry because the best room had been taken. She said that the room was hers and that the hotel had made a mistake. The lady became quite nasty.

Her protest made the man upset, but he did not yell. At last, he got the lady a room. It was not the best one, but she had to take it.

The Jolly Menu

Sandy had a long day. She went home with a plan to fix a ham. When she got home, the ham was still frozen! She had not defrosted it and now she did not have time. Her mind had been set on the ham.

She went into the pantry. She had plenty of meat left from the night before. Sandy did not wish to have the same exact thing, so she made a gravy to go with it.

Sandy's husband, Ted, came home. She told him that she was set to dine. The menu was not the best; the gravy was so lumpy! Ted was jolly and made jokes to console Sandy. She did not find it funny. Sandy still felt it was a shame not to have the ham.

Henry Retires

Henry was set to retire at sixty-five. At last, he could begin to relax. He did not mind at all. Henry had a tiny shop in his basement. He was a self-made man, quite handy with welding.

Henry had done plenty of work his entire life. He was glad to say farewell to it. He intended to recline the moment he sold his shop.

The shop sold quickly. Now he could spend his life-long savings. Henry had done his duty. Now he could fly south to an expensive hotel and take a long, long sunbath at last!

A

consonant	melody	galaxy
comprehend	develop	elastic
microscope	disrespect	opponent
impolite	enemy	educate
tuxedo	coconut	volcano

B

demolish	absolute	hydroplane
rejuvenate	despondent	obsolete
blazonry	electron	delinquent
espresso	regulate	isolate
humankind	stipulate	cohesive

invasive	evaluate	microscopic
romantic	represent	remodel
immunize	responsive	repulsive
economy	patronize	congregate
colonist	economize	explosive

diplomat	defensive	hemoglobin
electrode	retrospect	insulin
itemize	tabulate	stimulate
majesty	basketry	suffocate
faculty	soft-spoken	re-collect

incubate	egotist	dioxide
stipulate	strangulate	succulent
utensil	monopolize	open-minded
humanistic	humanize	monotone
patronize	amputate	accumulate

speculate	tonsillitis	molecule
kilogram	segregate	prolific
imprudent	exodus	uncanny
balcony	alfresco	document
amnesty	ebony	relinquish

agony	condensate	embassy
indolent	eloquent	redundant
absolute	dependent	pendulum
stipulate	confiscate	Astrodome
replenish	adhesive	exclusive

explosive	economic	delegate
diplomat	comedy	execute
accolade	immunize	impudent
gallantry	intrusive	occupant
inclusive	obsolete	populate

monotony	open-ended	renovate
obtrusive	pantomime	reprehend
panoramic	protocol	simulate
protrusive	retrofit	vitalize
replenish	monogram	agonize
requital	prohibit	antagonize
reflexive	reflective	devilry
industry	by-product	dyadic
penalize	retrograde	equivocate
deregulate	microstate	infantry

1   James likes to sing that melody to the baby.

2   Wendy will find all the consonants on this list.

3   The galaxy is so much fun to study.

4   Henry must rent a tuxedo for the prom.

5   This elastic will hold the lid on the box.

6   We can see this small object with a microscope.

7   Amy plans to develop her talent on skates.

8   Bill likes to munch on coconut candy.

9   It is impolite to stare.

10   We must develop a skit for the class.

1   Mr. Griffin must not violate his contract.

2   I think that frog's legs are repulsive to eat.

3   Jimmy went to the game to evaluate the opponent.

4   Tammy is so shy and soft-spoken but Betsy likes to monopolize a talk.

5   This faculty represents the best in the state.

6   That long-winded man spoke in monotone.

7   We must develop a plan to remodel our home.

8   I like to read romantic novels.

9   Mom dislikes the mess that can accumulate in the shed.

10   Mr. Smith's explosive protest made Tommy erupt.

1   I think this product is obsolete.

2   The economy was strong last month.

3   Did James win the all-inclusive trip?

4   We must renovate the old shed.

5   I must pass this math class to graduate.

6   I think the opponent has had extensive help.

7   Jenny was impolite to her dad in the lobby of the hotel.

8   Itemize the bill and send them a copy.

9   Could Congress regulate the cost of gas?

10   Jake represented Tom for the big case.

1   Pete rented a tuxedo to go to the prom.

2   Did Tom panic when he shot the elastic and it hit Mr. Cahill?

3   Hire a consultant to evaluate this program.

4   Jimmy will calculate the math problems before he goes to bed.

5   I hope that Betsy is open-minded when we discuss this problem.

6   The kids did not demolish the script.

7   We cannot isolate Tommy from the class.

8   A fantastic video club will open in the spring.

9   Ken is in agony over his loss.

10 The congressman would like to rejuvenate that old mill, but it would be too expensive.

1   Did the salesman discuss a novelty item?

2   Jake and Molly went out for espresso and hot, fresh, bran muffins.

3   Mr. Henry hopes to stimulate a state-wide program to assist the homeless.

4   James can assume the role of a diplomat.

5   The kids like to congregate at the donut shop.

6   Must we incubate these ostrich eggs?

7   A humanistic welfare program will help.

8   The state's economy is the best it has been in a long time.

9   The company's loss was reflective of a lack of sales.

10 The faculty will have a banquet.

1   The vital document was lost in the trash.

2   Mr. Fresno likes to speculate with stocks.

3   Rod and his date will dine alfresco.

4   This skyline balcony is so fantastic!

5   If you isolate my pup, she will be sad.

6   That open-ended statement made us think more about the immigrants.

7   Ellen is soft-spoken in math class.

8   We must care for this planet that we populate.

9   Stan has the exclusive copy of the script.

10   Adhesive tape can do the job well.

Equipment Problem

A conflict over the use of equipment became a problem at the Smith Company. The boss had neglected the problem until it became explosive. He then had to respond. At last, he did regulate the use of the equipment. He did not wish to do this, but he felt it would combat the problem.

People then had to complete a request for equipment time. This became an absolute requirement. People in the company were upset, but the boss insisted. In the end, it did help solve the conflict.

Jimmy and Betsy

Jimmy and Betsy did not have plans. They did not have company and so they were glad to just relax. Jimmy went to the video store and rented a romantic film for Betsy. They had plenty of junky refreshments.

Jimmy did not like the video. He felt that it was silly. Betsy did not evaluate it so badly. She felt that it was OK. Still, they had a fun night. It felt good to just recline and be lazy.

The Explosive Volcano

The siren blasted at nine a.m. All those native to the remote land had expected it. The destructive volcano had erupted. A plan had been made to evacuate and now there was no time left to prepare. People had to vacate their homes. Despite the plan, many did not wish to go, but they had to escape the hot, explosive lava.

Tommy Strum

The faculty at the Miltone High School was quite upset with Tommy Strum. He was defiant. He was impolite to the teachers and, at times, explosive. His disrespect made the teachers want to expel him.

Tommy did not care about the content of his classes. He did not fulfill the requirements. Most times he did not even attend.

Tommy did like to violate all the rules. He disrupted his classes, and the teachers felt they could not educate him until he committed himself to school. His mom and dad were insistent that he stop his delinquent ways.

a

Donna	extra	antenna
umbrella	Atlanta	Sandra
vanilla	awhile	alone
alive	awoke	amaze
Alaska	Apollo	amuse

i

substitute	difficult	confident
hesitate	apricot	domino
compliment	continent	gravity
cabinet	cavity	animal
president	investigate	festival

a=/ə/

stigma	comma	villa
ultra	tundra	toga
vista	delta	stanza
dogma	henna	Kenya
alfalfa	yucca	Calcutta

a=/ə/

fibula	quota	scuba
gala	rotunda	credenza
yoga	vendetta	chinchilla
atomic	abuse	adapt
amid	aloft	abandon

a = /ə/

acute	anemic	abide
agaze	aside	abode
atone	abolish	arise
aline	adept	awaken
manipulate	kabob	manila

i = /ə/ or /ĭ/

attitude	sensitive	acclimate
stabilize	estimate	subsidize
subsidy	indirect	platitude
fumigate	platinum	mutilate
scrutinize	bassinet	lubricate

i=/ə/ or /ĭ/

manicure	halibut	subdivide
duplicate	instigate	silicone
implicate	sanitize	nominate
minimize	optimum	mobilize
medicate	imitate	dominate

i=/ə/ or /ĭ/

litigate	sentiment	antiquate
abstinent	maximize	altitude
antidote	cultivate	applicant
complicate	indicate	denigrate
oxidize	magnitude	obligate

dignity	candidate	ventilate
fabricate	detriment	amplitude
entity	condiment	palpitate
culminate	pessimist	supplicant
destiny	meditate	radical

pollinate	primitive	imitate
chastity	applicant	indigo
attribute	cultivate	vanity
denizen	sentinel	cannibal
manifold	resident	multitude

i = /ə/ or /ĭ/

gratitude	episode	activate
cannibal	dedicate	epidemic
emigrate	evident	gallivant
comical	optimize	litigate
habitat	brevity	liquidate

i = /ə/ or /ĭ/

liniment	imminent	optimist
oxidize	penitent	plenitude
politics	practical	punitive
reprimand	rudiment	ruminate
utilize	validate	vindicate

i=/ə/ or /ĭ/

ventilate	dividend	minimum
institute	captivate	ridicule
magnitude	cognizant	confidant
crepitate	criminal	illuminate
optimistic	discriminate	contaminate

i=/ə/ or /ĭ/

amenity	intoxicate	consolidate
invalidate	assassinate	eliminate
aluminum	humility	insensitive
eliminate	intoxicant	utility
manipulate	illuminate	invalidate

a=/ə/

1   Donna will finish this job in awhile.

2   I plan to get a vanilla milk shake.

3   The state of Alaska has lots of frozen tundra.

4   The baby awoke and began to cry.

5   Did that trick amaze the class?

6   Evan lost the antenna to his van in the crash.

7   Betsy did not bring her umbrella and now she regrets it!

8   The club will fly on a Delta jet to Atlanta.

9   Timmy insists that he will have extra time to visit his mom.

10 Tim's instinct did amaze me.

i=/ə/ or /ĭ/

1   Sandra likes to go to the festival.

2   Rosa is the class president.

3   We must act now and not hesitate.

4   The dentist will drill my cavity.

5   Get the domino set on the top shelf.

6   Jessica likes all the animals in the pet shop.

7   We have had a substitute in class now for quite awhile.

8   Can you name the seven continents?

9   Kendra had to go to the hospital.

10   That cabinet is a mess!

a=/ə/

1 Donna must submit the script to Mr. Kimes.

2 Sally will complete the last stanza of her song.

3 Sandy will discuss the trip to Kenya at the club.

4 Tammy likes to add alfalfa to her salad.

5 The boss did not think we could make the sales quota, but we did.

6 Ed rented a villa in the French hills.

7 Mr. Lang insisted that we abide by the rules.

8 The students from the academy will compete in the statewide contest.

9 Edna will go take scuba lessons before she goes on her trip.

10 Anna has to get vanilla so she can make the cupcakes.

a=/ə/ | i=/ə/ or /ĭ/

1 Sandra will invite Mohammed to the gala event.

2 Our company plans to abandon that product line.

3 We still cannot adapt to our new boss.

4 The problem arose when the prospective sale did not happen.

5 With the conflict aside, Jim and Susanna can begin the task.

6 If you come in late, take care not to awaken the children.

7 Despite the problem, the boss hopes to duplicate the sales.

8 We must ventilate the basement.

9 Russel is confident in Edna's ability as boss.

10 Mr. Banty is such an optimistic man, but his wife is so pessimistic.

i=/ə/ or /ĭ/

1 Dave gave Sandra a compliment that made her blush.

2 The democratic candidate will visit this school.

3 If Melissa takes time off now, it will complicate this mess even more!

4 I hope there is a way to ventilate the attic.

5 Beth's sensitive skin broke out in a rash.

6 Did Tommy nominate you for class president?

7 Glen plans to attend that institute and take up welding.

8 Mohammed is the best applicant for the job.

9 Did the baby try to imitate Jimmy?

10 It is difficult for Katy to ask for help; she is so shy.

i=/ə/ or /ĭ/

1   The salesman will estimate the cost and then give us a call.

2   Did the gals spend the cash for a manicure?

3   Lenny did not instigate the conflict.

4   Grandma must use an old antidote to save the puppy from the snakebite.

5   Did you indicate the problem when you spoke to him?

6   Mr. Gannon likes to debate politics.

7   The humming bird helps to pollinate those lilacs.

8   The magnitude of the problem is evident.

9   That gas will contaminate the pond.

10   We must utilize all of our help.

ī=/ə/ or /ĭ/

1   Lakesha did a comical act for the class.

2   Mrs. Sanchez plans to eliminate that program.

3   I hope this flu does not become an epidemic.

4   Collect the aluminum cans and drop them into the bin at the dump.

5   You must not discriminate.

6   Can you dedicate this next song to Sandy?

7   I think that episode is a rerun.

8   Validate your ticket at a shop in the mall.

9   Mike Rosa is an optimistic man.

10 Mrs. Costanza will reprimand the child.

Golden Skates

Anna did hope to go to the Olympics for the U.S.A. She had spent so much of her life at the rink! She could skate well and was in tip-top shape. When Anna made the team, she had to prepare. She could not relax much. Anna was athletic and talented as well as intensive about her work. She had to be optimistic about her ability to win.

When Anna was a contestant, she was confident. She could captivate the people in the stands. Anna had plenty of fans that would respond to her difficult stunts. It was a thrill to see her skate.

The prospect of a gold medal gave Anna her drive. People predicted that she could possibly finish second. Her best opponent was from Finland. So much depended on the last event. A drastic mistake or even a small slip would effect the result. (continued)

Golden Skates (continued)

Anna had one last skate and she could win the gold. She chose a song with a fast tempo. The fans began to clap as she began to glide across the ice. The fans in the arena sat in amazement when she did the difficult jumps. She was fantastic! The fans were explosive at the finish.

Anna did try her best for the gold. At last, the moment came. Anna had won the gold medal for the U.S.A! Anna went to shake hands with the gal from Finland. Then she began to cry just a bit as she gave a big wave to the fans who were clapping wildly for her. The thrill was more than she had ever dreamed.

Mrs. Rosa for President

Mrs. Rosa hopes to become the next president of the local business club. She has an optimistic attitude and it is evident that many people like her. She presents a positive plan for the community.

Mrs. Rosa does not like politics but she has to mobilize people to get votes. Her opponent is a strong candidate as well. Mrs. Rosa will need lots of help to eliminate him and win. She plans to get the maximum number of votes but to do it without unjustly attacking her opponent.

Posttest Step 5

gravy	Apollo	defend
continent	plenty	shy
elastic	provide	prevent
alone	flu	umbrella
rotate	extra	galaxy

hydrate	diplomat	crusade
document	spry	tundra
rodent	sultry	amnesty
awaken	Atlanta	amplitude
delinquent	optimist	deduct

Posttest Step 5

stry	triden	prespere
cre	po	spanty
blenet	belna	shipe
rebect	flothine	ploton
promitive	stomest	crozump

1 Divide words into syllables.

2 Mark syllables: open, closed, v-e, and open exceptions.

3 Mark the sound of the vowel **y**.

NOTES